Feng Shui Workbook for Teens

Feng Shui Workbook for Teens

Amie Crouch

Writer's Showcase
New York Lincoln Shanghai

Feng Shui Workbook for Teens

Writer's Showcase
an imprint of iUniverse, Inc.

For information address:
iUniverse
2021 Pine Lake Road, Suite 100
Lincoln, NE 68512
www.iuniverse.com

ISBN: 0-595-26061-6 (Pbk)
ISBN: 0-595-65513-0 (Cloth)

Printed in the United States of America

This book was written with the hope that every teenager will see the infinite possibilities they can create for themselves in this abundant universe.

I would like to thank my family and friends for all the support they have given me throughout the writing of this book. Special thanks to my husband Todd, my mother Sara, Sue Chartrand, and Jamie Robertson.

CONTENTS

WELCOME TO
FENG SHUI FOR TEENS!

I can't wait for you to get started on your exciting journey toward peace and balance. This book is designed as a workbook that will enable you to make changes in your environment right away. You will learn the basic Feng Shui principles and are encouraged to add your personal creativity and style along the way. Enjoy!

CHAPTER ONE

Feng Shui: Why Is It Important?

Why is Feng Shui important to those in their adolescent years? If you think about it, Feng Shui makes a lot of sense. Learning some simple strategies of balance and rearranging will help these years be some of the best of your life. For example, if you start by working with your "home base" (bedroom) and create a harmonious environment, then you can face all other areas of your life with a positive, healthy attitude. It is important to learn to balance your own living area. You can create a peaceful, personalized space you feel comfortable in that will reflect your personality. This book will teach you how to analyze and make important adjustments to bring happiness into your life. Applying Feng Shui principles in your living area is relatively simple.

Once you create a balanced environment, you will be able to better focus on who you really are and what makes you truly happy. You will be amazed at how your self-esteem will start to soar as you begin to get things done and start attracting positive energy and people into your life. As a teenager you may be thinking about:

- Maintaining good grades and finding a decent place to study
- Developing a healthy, independent relationship with parents
- Building friendships with supportive people
- Learning about relationships
- Deciding on a college or career

- Finding clothes that make you feel confident and reflect success
- Making personal time
- Getting the right part-time job
- Planning your successful future

Dealing with these things can be easier if you have an organized and balanced environment. This means your locker at school, your car, and your room need to be balanced. We are going to learn about Feng Shui principles and do hands-on exercises that will allow you to make changes.

Remember how it feels when everything in the world seems so peaceful and just right in your life? The goal is to create a place that gives you that same feeling, so that you build friendships and interact with significant others with greater confidence. This book is designed as a creative tool that can make a difference in your life.

 *Feng Shui literally means "wind and water." Wind and water play such an important part in our lives that we would not survive without either one. Feng Shui is the study of how the energy from wind and water affects us and how we can effectively use that energy to create a great life for ourselves.*

Feng Shui, pronounced fung shway, is not new; it has been around for about 6,000 years. The key to Feng Shui is to balance energy, known as "chi," in a way that creates positive changes in your environment. The Chinese believe that using Feng Shui principles will allow us to create harmonious living conditions leading to health, wealth, and happiness. This workbook just scratches the surface of the complex study of Feng Shui. Think of this as an introduction.

There are numerous classes, lectures, books, and programs you can visit to learn about the more complicated aspects of this fascinating study. You can share your knowledge with friends and family. These principles apply to them as well. Let's get started!

You Create Personal Luck

In Feng Shui, the Chinese focus on three types of luck: earth luck, heaven luck, and human luck. Each is supposed to make up one-third of your life.

- Heaven luck represents the situation in which you were born. For example, being part of a wealthy family brings with it certain gifts as well as challenges. Inheriting athletic talent can benefit those with an interest in sports.

- Earth luck is the environment around you on the planet. You can use Feng Shui to improve your physical surroundings to make your environment more appealing.

- Human luck is a culmination of the decisions you make every day. How good or bad are they? Deciding not to study for the final in Algebra can help determine your success in the course. In that sense, you help make your own luck.

What can you do differently to change your luck? You can make a difference with earth luck and human luck.

To change your human luck, start by setting goals for your future. They can be large or small. Think about something you have always wanted to do, that you feel passionate about, and find a way to do it. If it takes money you don't have, then start a savings plan until you reach your goal. Look into taking lessons, check out online courses, learn a hobby from a friend, or volunteer to be a camp counselor. You can shape your future by your attitude and strong commitment to what you believe. Don't be afraid to try something new. Expand your knowledge base and doors will open! See for yourself as you learn ways to enhance your environment.

You can change your earth luck with Feng Shui. When you start to do the exercises in this book, you can make your environment more conducive to positive energy so that all aspects of your life can benefit.

Creating Abundance

If you truly want a lifestyle that makes you happy and creates abundance, the negative influences around you need to be eliminated as much as possible. This includes your own negativity. Have you heard of the old saying that some people look at life as a cup half full and others look at life as a cup half empty? How you view things is really important. Looking at life as a cup half full is the way we want to be. Just looking at things in a positive way helps create positive energy.

As you start to work on your physical surroundings to make them more in line with the universe, this is also a good time to look inward. Every day you create karma by your actions, which can be positive or negative. Karma is a universal rule that means there is a reaction to every action. Positive actions result in positive reactions. Negative actions result in negative reactions, maybe not at once, but eventually. For example, when you notice someone wearing clothes you would not be caught dead wearing, and you find yourself filled with critical comments, keep in mind that this same event could happen to you. Practice changing your thinking to focus on the positive.

Remember, if we were all alike, life would be boring. It is so easy to find fault in others when we should be celebrating our differences. Next time you see someone and you notice something about him or her that you genuinely like, say so! Notice how great that makes you feel inside. You are creating positive karma in your life. Throwing out positives brings those positives back to you. Think of it as a boomerang effect.

Think about getting to know a person who is not like you. Find out what makes that person tick. You may be surprised how much you learn about yourself in the process. Avoid being caught in a fishbowl where you limit yourself to a select group of people. Also, if you are hanging out with a group that promotes gossiping, then you may want to take a good look at your friends. Gossip is the biggest breeder of negativity, so let it stop with you. You will be surprised how much trust people will start to have in you.

Think abundantly and create your own reality.

Remember to keep things in perspective. Issues you have now won't seem so big later, so look at them as if they were pebbles in the road. The important thing is to make sure you are your own support system and realize how much of a difference you can make in your own life. Take a few minutes to evaluate yourself at least once a month. List the things you do well and things you would like to improve. Set a goal based on a strength and a weakness. Use this self-study as a fun way to take a look at yourself.

Things I am good at: *Example: babysitting*	Things I would like to improve: *Example: being on time*
1.	1.
2.	2.
3.	3.

Now, let's set a goal. Choose one thing you do well and one thing you would like to improve. Make sure your choice is realistic and not impossible to reach. Use the goal-setting sheet to guide you. First, state your goal by saying, "I will do..." This ensures you are serious about your goal and that it is positive.

Next, your goal must be desirable. This is particularly important when you first start setting goals because you won't be successful unless you really want to do it. Finally, your goal must be measurable so that you will know when you have achieved it. So instead of saying, "I'd like to be a good student," say, "I will turn in all of my assignments completed and on time."

It is important to know exactly what it will take to complete your goal. Go one step further and list the specific activities you will do to reach your goal. For example:

Desired Goal:	I would like to be an "A" student.
Action step #1	Spend three extra hours studying on Sunday morning starting December 1.
Action step #2	Find a math tutor in two weeks.
Action step #3	Make a list of upcoming tests.
Action step #4	Enroll a family member to quiz me on possible test questions starting two weeks before test.

Now you have set yourself up for success by creating a plan of action! Remember, do this same process periodically so you have current goals and action plans in the works.

Desired Goal:	
Action step #1	
Action step #2	
Action step #3	

Goal-Setting Exercise #1

Set a goal that can be accomplished within two weeks. State your goal in positive terms, and be specific.

I will _____.

Make sure you follow the criteria for effective goal setting:

1. My goal is realistic.   Yes__ No__

2. My goal is stated positively.   Yes__ No__

3. My goal is desirable.   Yes__ No__

4. My goal is measurable.   Yes__ No__

What can you tell yourself to help you be successful with your goal?

_____

Who could support you in accomplishing this goal?

_____

Note:

Don't worry what other people think; follow your heart. Nothing is more attractive than people who have a positive attitude and interesting things going on in their lives.

CHAPTER TWO

Working with Your Bedroom

"Have nothing in your houses that you do not know to be useful or believe to be beautiful."

—William Morris English Designer

One of the basic rules of Feng Shui is to live and work in an environment that is free of clutter. You need to take a long hard look at what you have and decide if it belongs in your life. The following exercise will help you reevaluate and purge what you don't need and get you ready for a fresh new start.

We are going to think of each area as a section for success.

Declutter Exercise

1. Stand in the doorway of your room with a pen and paper. Draw an outline of your room and include the placement of your bed, dresser, closet, desk, and any other items you have in your room. If you have a space that is your "get ready area" in the morning, then draw it on your personal floor plan.
2. Look at every area objectively and use these rules for each section:
   Do I love the things in that area? Does it make me happy when I see it, or does it remind me of a past experience that wasn't posi-

tive? Having a stuffed animal from an old relationship sitting right on your bed will only remind you of that person every time you see it. Is that a thought you want running through your head on a daily basis?

Surround yourself with positive things that make you feel good when you see them. We'll show you how to give some things away that eliminate negative energy from your room while adding to someone else's life.

3. Do I need it? Have I used it (or worn it) within the past year? (This will include clothes, so get ready.) Consider that miniskirt or old pair of jeans you have been saving that just might fit or be in style someday. Give it to a thrift store and when you have some extra money, buy something new that you can enjoy wearing now.

4. Do I have things that don't belong to me that I have been meaning to return? Return whatever it is to the rightful owner immediately. You will be surprised at how this frees your mind from those lingering "to do's." Give yourself until the end of the week to return the items. Make sure you get it done.

You will notice that piles will start to form. Get strong trash bags and divide all of your excess stuff into these labeled bags:

Trash   Recycling

Thrift Store   Items to return to owner

Hand-me-downs

Make sure you plan on taking care of the distribution of these piles immediately! Leaving them sitting for days or weeks on end will spoil the whole plan for success and positive change, blocking the flow of good chi in the room! We will discuss chi and how it affects your space in a later chapter.

General Rule of Abundance:

By giving to the universe great gifts will come your way!

Your bedroom should be a place you can go to rest and to rejuvenate your spirit. Make sure you create an atmosphere that is comfortable and enjoyable.

Mirrors

If you use a mirror in the bedroom, make sure it does not reflect the bed. Your sleeping area is a place to unwind and relax. Having your image reflected in a mirror when you are trying to sleep creates disruptive energy.

If you use a mirror to get dressed, make sure it is on the inside of a closet door. A small makeup mirror is okay so long as it doesn't reflect the bed.

Another rule for using mirrors in any part of the house is to be careful of what they reflect. They should reflect a positive view of nature or water, not disturbing shapes or a cluttered area.

Bed

When you are deciding where to place your bed, make sure it is supported by a solid wall and is diagonal from the bedroom door. To get the most restful sleep, place your bed where you can see the door, but not directly in line with it. Also, be careful not to place your bed directly under a window because it could disturb your sleep.

Ashley, a teenager in Iowa, has her bed directly under a window and does not have trouble sleeping. The reason is that the window is located very high up and she has a solid wall behind her bed giving her support. She also is sleeping in one of her good directions (we will cover directions in a later chapter), which is more important than sleeping under a window.

Having a great view outside your bedroom window is a Feng Shui bonus. It is amazing how having a visually positive environment around us can affect our outlook on life.

Note:

If you don't have a great view, get creative, find some material, and make some cool curtains to liven up the view. You can place a poster of a beautiful nature scene on the wall if you need to. Sometimes just a square of material can be twisted and wrapped around the curtain rod to look great.

Electronics in the Bedroom

Any item in your room that is electrical will stimulate the energy in your room. The bedroom is supposed to be a place to unwind and relax, so these stimulants are not recommended. Try to keep your computer in another room in the house. If you have to have a television in your bedroom, cover the screen with a cloth when you are not using it to cut down on some of the reflection. This will reduce disruptive energy.

Eliminating these electrical influences can increase the amount of harmony in your bedroom.

It has been said that a shark will never out-  grow its environment. If you put it in a pond it'll grow only a few feet, but put it in the ocean and it'll grow to be twenty feet long. If you want to grow, you have to change your environment.

CHAPTER THREE

The Basic Components of Feng Shui

What Is Chi?

Chi is the energy that flows through everything in life. The key of Feng Shui is to balance energy known as chi pronounced (chee) in a way that creates positive changes in your environment. Chi is invisible, but you can see the way it flows through all of the empty space in your room. Think of the furniture as rocks and the empty space as water (chi), and picture how it would move through your room.

When you have chi that flows in straight lines, the effect on your environment can be negative. You also might feel stuck or unmotivated. Feng Shui practitioners call chi that flows in straight lines "poison arrows." Think about how important it is to have good energy around you and how that would make you feel. Good Feng Shui is dependent on how much chi is present.

How do you get more chi? The Declutter Exercise was a great first step in increasing the amount of chi in your room. Remember that any form of excessive clutter will stop the healthy flow of chi. Plus, we can declutter our bodies as well as our environment.

*People do tai chi and yoga
to help chi flow through the body.*

Tai chi has been practiced in China for centuries. It is a study that teaches you how to move and breathe so you can improve the energy flow within your body. This improves flexibility, relaxation, and strength. Take a class at a nearby gym or a local college and see for yourself. Yoga and Pilates classes are also great ways to work with your energies to improve balance, flexibility and strength.

Chi-Enhancing Tips

- Make sure you have a gentle, circular pattern for chi to flow between furniture and other things in your room. If you don't think you have a good flow, move furniture around to create a more positive arrangement.
- Find the empty corners in a room. Try to have an object or something that will round your corners, encouraging the circular flow of chi.
- If you have a school locker, make sure it is organized. It is not beneficial for your papers to fly out everywhere when you open it. Having to deal with a mess a couple of times a day can be draining on your energy. You want to have all areas of your life clear of clutter to invite chi to move gently through.
- Using live plants in your home is great, but be careful not to have an excess in the bedroom. During the day they take in carbon dioxide and produce oxygen, but at night they compete with us for oxygen.
- If you have dried flowers in your room, make sure they are dust-free and that you change them out for new ones regularly. Old flowers can bring stale energy into your space. Autumn, a teenager in Colorado, had multiple clumps of dried flowers hanging from her ceiling that

she wanted to save. Removing the flowers allowed fresh energy to circulate throughout the room.

Wind chimes in general enhance the amount of chi in a room because they generate sound waves. They all have a unique sound and can be very relaxing and comforting.

Get a wind chime if you feel like your room has stagnant energy. These sound waves will help create more energy. If you are hanging one in your bedroom, place it high enough so that visitors do not run into it.

The best type of wind chime has hollow rods to help let the chi in. If you have a lot going on in your room already, and have trouble concentrating, think twice about adding a wind chime.

Hanging beads in your doorway is another way you can enhance the amount of chi in your room. The movement from the beads when people enter through the door will generate more chi. What a great way to create a whole new look without actually removing your bedroom door! Just tack the beads to the top of the door frame.

Case Studies

Liz, a teenager from Missouri, originally had her furniture flush against the wall. Her desk was facing the wall and her bed was under a window. She said that this arrangement was okay but did not feel quite right. She had trouble sleeping. It was recommended that she move her bed out from under the window (the window was located low enough to create disruptive chi) so she would have a solid backing for her bed. She had some empty corners that she filled to create a circular, positive flow of chi in her bedroom. She is very happy with the result and feels more peaceful. She is also able to sleep better.

Perry, a teenager in Colorado, had old, dried-up flowers on his desk that his girlfriend had given him. He was relieved when the suggestion was made to throw them out or save them in a memory box. He also had a lot of papers and model rocket boxes stacked under his desk table. The stack was moved to the closet and he said he felt like he had more space and did not feel as closed in.

Note:

Make sure the plants you surround yourself with have rounded leaves. Plants with sharp and pointed leaves put out negative energy. One of the worst plants to have is the cactus.

Floor Plan Exercise

Write down the location of all your furniture in the space below. Don't worry if it isn't perfect; it will give you an idea of how your personal chi is flowing. Think about what changes you can make. Remember, the goal is to allow chi to move and breathe around your furniture.

Chi-Enhancing Checklist
1. Find the empty corners in your bedroom and fill them.
2. Analyze the placement of your furniture to make sure chi flows in a circular pattern.
3. Check areas for clutter.
4. Make sure your bed is not under a window.

Personal Floor Plan

Yin and Yang

Tai Chi
The yin and yang symbol is said to resemble two fish gliding together.

Now you should have a grasp of the concept of chi and how it works in your environment. We are going to take things one step further and talk about yin and yang. Chi energy can be either yin or yang.

In the diagram at the top of the page, notice how yin and yang are opposites, yet dependent on one another. There is a little bit of yin in yang and little bit of yang in yin. This illustrates the balance of both in your surroundings.

Yang	Yin
Light	Dark
Hot	Cold
Day	Night
Male	Female

If you have too much yang (light), you might feel like you never follow through with a project or assignment. The light colors might give you too much stimulation and make it hard to concentrate. If you have too much yin (dark), you might feel depressed or weighed down. The dark colors can also make you sleepy.

Look around your room and make a list of objects that fall under yin or yang. For example:

Yang	Yin
cream comforter	dark wood desk
yellow candles	Indian print blanket
light-colored lampshade	dark green velvet pillows
light-colored chair	dark poster

If you notice that your list of yin items is longer than your yang items, that's okay. The Chinese believe it is better to have more yin in the bedroom because it is a place for rest and rejuvenation.

Yin/Yang Analysis for All Rooms

Yin Objects	Yang Objects
1.	1.
2.	2.
3.	3.
4.	4.
5.	5.
6.	6.
7.	7.
8.	8.
9.	9.
10.	10.

Do this exercise for all appropriate rooms, your car, and your locker.

Bedroom Wall Colors

When you are thinking about colors to paint your bedroom, think yin colors instead of yang colors. Remember that the bedroom is a place to unwind and get a good night's sleep. Bright bold colors may not allow you to relax, especially if you have posters or other items hanging on your wall.

If your walls are bright white, make sure they are not over stimulating. You might want to try a softer shade of white or off-white because the color is less active.

When you are at a friend's house or in a store, notice how the different wall coloring affects your mood and make a mental note. Find some decorating magazines and cut out pictures of rooms that you could see yourself living in. Keep them in a file or notebook.

Some studies have linked the power of color to mood. Red, for example, can lead to stress and anxiety. Green can produce calm, and blue can produce serenity. Prison studies have shown that a pink room is calm in the beginning but produces stress later. Light yellow is uplifting. Notice the effect of different colors on your and your family's moods.

Note:

The color red can be over stimulating. Red can wear a person out and lead to anxiety because of its intensity. Stick to calm colors if possible, such as cream, pink, beige, light blue, or purple. Colors can make a difference in your thinking.

Five Elements

Everything around us is made up of five elements. These five elements are wood, fire, earth, metal, and water. They each represent types of energies that are found on earth. They are often referred to as the children of yin and yang.

The goal is to have a balance between the elements in your living space because they can affect your luck. The five elements naturally react to one another, and should work in your environment in a harmonious and productive way.

The Productive Cycle you see below shows how the elements should work together in your environment. Naturally, it makes sense that the elements would have this effect on each other.

Productive Cycle

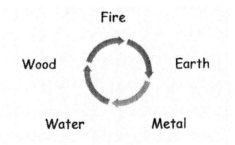

Fire

Wood   Earth

Water   Metal

- Wood produces Fire.
- Fire leaves behind Earth (ash).
- Earth is the source of Metal.
- Metal liquefies into Water.
- Water helps Wood to thrive.

Here are some examples of things you might have in your room and the elements they represent.

Fire Element	Earth Element	Metal Element
red lava lamp	yellow comforter	white walls
candles	square storage crate	metal picture frame

Water Element	Wood Element
mirror	green fountain plants
blue pillows	

If your environment does not feel right, it is usually because of a missing or clashing element. This is easy to fix!

If you are missing an element, your environment will usually feel unbalanced. You might not be able to put your finger on it, but something just doesn't feel right. Elements in nature can work destructively against one another. The arrows show this in the Domination Cycle on the next page. Look at the element fire and how it melts metal; you need to add the element between the two clashing ones (earth) to restore the balance in your environment. Another example is how metal cuts wood, so you need to add something to represent the water element to restore the natural cycle.

So, as a general rule of thumb:

If you have Fire and Metal, add Earth.

If you have Earth and Water, add Metal.

If you have Metal and Wood, add Water.

If you have Water and Fire, add Wood.

If you have Wood and Earth, add Fire.

Domination Cycle

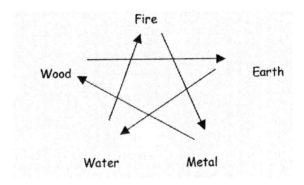

• Wood draws nutrients from Earth.

• Fire melts Metal.

• Earth blocks or dams Water.

• Metal cuts Wood.

• Water puts out Fire.

Examples of Clashing Elements

1. If you have a water fountain (water element) and candles (fire element) in your room, make sure you have plants or something the color green (wood element) to balance the clashing elements.

2. Shannon has a lot of metal picture frames (metal element) in her room. She also has several plants in her room (wood element). The room

has good energy because she has a humidifier (water element) that balances the clashing energy of metal and wood.

Five-Element Exercise

Walk around your room and list items under the element category they represent. Refer to the chart below to help you determine where something belongs. After you are finished making the list, you can determine if your elements are balanced. If you don't have anything listed under water, then you know you need to add something to balance the wood and metal (wood cuts metal) to restore the productive cycle.

Fire Element	Earth Element	Metal Element
1.	1.	1.
2.	2.	2.
3.	3.	3.
4.	4.	4.
5.	5.	5.

Water Element	Wood Element
1.	1.
2.	2.
3.	3.
4.	4.
5.	5.

Remember:

- Fire leaves behind Earth (ash).
- Earth is the source of Metal.
- Metal liquefies into Water.
- Water helps Wood to thrive.
- Wood produces Fire.

The five elements are listed below with the corresponding color, shape, or item that represents each one. Use this chart when you are making your list of elements and you can work on balancing your space.

Five-Element Chart

	Element	Color	Shape	What To Use
	Wood	green, brown, blue		bamboo, plants, flowers
	Fire	red, purple		color red, candles, red lamp shade
	Earth	yellow, earth tones		terra cotta pots, ceramic, stones, real crystals
	Metal	pastels, white, silver, gold		metal-framed pictures, wind chimes
	Water	black, dark blue, burgundy		fountain, humidifier, aquariums, mirrors, glass

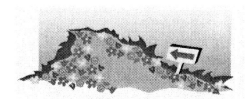

Five-Element Scavenger Hunt

Explore the outdoors to see firsthand how the five elements naturally interact in your environment. Find a park or recreation area and explore. You can get so distracted in life that an afternoon to get back in touch with nature may be just what you need to get yourself out of the every-day routine. Make it a serious day to connect with the outdoors in a way that will help you learn to apply the elements to your life.

Get ready:
Call a friend.
Bring a backpack.
Pack a lunch.
Bring your journal.
Wear comfortable hiking shoes.

Look for the five elements (fire, earth, metal, wood, and water) in the natural environment. Notice how they are a part of everything around you. Here is a list of things to look for:

Fire	Earth	Metal	Water	Wood
Color red	Stones	Circular shapes	Lake or pond	Flowers
Triangular shapes	Earth tones	Metal signs	Wavy shapes	Natural wood

Note:

An afternoon retreat can reenergize you and help you keep things in perspective. Use the table to record your observations.

Table of Observations

Date	Fire	Earth	Metal	Water	Wood
2/10	red flower	soil	iron bench	fountain	plants

You might want to put a collection of these observations in a journal, conducting your hunts on different days and in different locations. Examples are:

1. In a field
2. By a creek or lake
3. On a nature trail
4. On a farm
5. In the city
6. In the mountains

Personal Directions

Everyone has a personal number associated with his or her birth year. This number is called your "personal gua number," and is important because it will let you know the directions that are favorable or unfavorable for you. This will determine the direction you sleep, the direction you face while at work, and the best direction for a door in your bedroom or dorm room.

Think back to a time when you rearranged your room, and it looked great but something didn't feel right. You might have had trouble sleeping or concentrating when you studied, so you probably moved it back the way it was. Certain directions feel better to us than others. You can find out what directions are associated with your birth year in this chapter. First you have to calculate your personal gua number based on the year you were born.

"Gua" is a name for the number that corresponds with your birth year.

The Chinese lunar calendar is used instead of the regular calendar to figure out your personal gua number. The Chinese Lunar calendar is based on cycles of the moon. The American calendar (Gregorian calendar) is based on cycles of the sun. This is why the Chinese celebrate New Year's Day on a different day each year. Sometimes New Year's Day might be

February 5, so if your birthday were on February 3, you would use the year before the year you were born. Consult the Chinese calendar on the next page to find out what year to use to calculate your personal gua number. If your birthday falls between January 1 and February 4, you would still use the previous year instead of the New Year. For example, if you were born on January 15, 1988, you would use 1987 as your birth year instead of 1988 to calculate your gua number.

Here is a little history: Businesses in China close for a week at the end of each year. This time is reserved for families to get together and celebrate what happened during that year. New Year's Eve especially is a night for close family to get together and pay tribute to the passing of another year. In the Chinese culture, house cleaning is not allowed on New Year's Day because this is a time reserved for good spirits to come into homes. Cleaning on this day might disrupt the spirits. All of the cleaning is done prior to New Year's Day.

On the third day of the New Year, the Chinese do things to officially welcome the beginning of a year. They spend time with extended family, bringing them gifts (such as a bag of oranges) to wish them health, wealth, and prosperity. Firecrackers are sometimes used to clear out old chi and scare away mean spirits.

Chinese Lunar Calendar

Year Born	Lunar Year Starts	Year Born	Lunar Year Starts
1980	February 16	1997	February 7
1981	February 5	1998	January 28
1982	January 25	1999	February 16
1983	February 13	2000	February 5

1984	February 2	2001	January 24
1985	February 20	2002	February 12
1986	February 9	2003	February 1
1987	January 29	2004	January 22
1988	February 17	2005	February 9
1989	February 6	2006	January 29
1990	January 27	2007	February 18
1991	February 15	2008	February 7
1992	February 4	2009	January 26
1993	January 23	2010	February 14
1994	February 10	2011	February 3
1995	January 31	2012	January 23
1996	February 19	2013	February 10

Calculating Your Gua Number

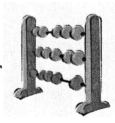

Add the last two numbers of your birth year until you have a single number.

For example, 1987: 8 + 7 = 15
Reduce the number further: 1 + 5 = 6

Girls: Add the above number to 5.
(i.e., 6 + 5 = 11; add again: 1 + 1 = 2)

Your personal gua number is 2.

Boys: Subtract the above number from 10.
(i.e., 10 - 6 = 4)

Your personal gua number is 4.

*If you were born in the year 2000, girls would add the number 6 (instead of 5) and boys would subtract from the number 9 (instead of 10).

Look at the chart below and find out what directions are associated with your gua number.

EAST LIFE
Gua number's 1, 3, 4, and 9

Best Directions   **Worst Directions**
Southeast   Southwest
South   West
North   Northeast
East   Northwest

WEST LIFE
Gua number's 2, 6, 7, and 8

Best Directions   **Worst Directions**
Northeast   North
West   South
Northwest   East
Southwest   Southeast

How to Use Personal Directions

Your personal directions labeled "good" are the best directions for you to use whenever possible. If you are interviewing for a job as a camp counselor or for a summer internship at a theme park, try to face one of your four best directions.

Try this: This exercise will help you apply your gua number to your area of sleep. Lie down on your bed and notice what direction your head is pointed. Take out your compass and determine what direction that is. This direction should be one of your four good directions. If it isn't, try rearranging your bed so that when you are lying down, your head points toward a good direction. Make sure you can still see the door from your bed. The most important thing is that you are not in the direct path of the door. If you can't get your head in your best direction, you can sleep diagonally, or in whatever position is most comfortable.

You can also use your personal directions to benefit you when you study. Try to face one of your good directions when you are sitting at your desk. Experiment and see if you can tell the difference!

The direction of your bedroom door can also determine how much positive chi you have. To find out your door direction, stand in the doorway to your room and face out, as if you were walking out the door. Check your direction chart and see if it is facing in one of your four good directions. If not, then see if you can convince a family member to switch. If you are selecting a dorm room, you can check out the door direction and see if it is positive before you move in.

Note:

Place your compass on a flat surface (like a hardcover book) to take a compass reading. You want to use a flat and steady surface to help you obtain a more reliable reading.

Chapter Four

College Applications

Deciding on a College

Choosing a college is never an easy decision. There are many factors to consider, so it is good to think about this early. Here are some of the things to consider. Do you want to go to an in-state or out-of-state college? Regardless of your answer, start doing some research. Find out what scholarships are available and what the academic requirements are for admission.

Have a meeting with your parents and discuss your plans, then make a top five list based on your personal finances and grades. Get on the computer and see what the campus looks like and send away for an information packet.

It is important to plan ahead for such a big goal. Try not to get caught at the last minute wondering what you want to do, only to find out that you could have had a lot more choices.

Setting yourself up for a successful future is all about affecting your human luck in a positive way.

Here are some guidelines for you to follow:

1. Make an appointment with your guidance counselor and talk about your college needs.

2. Make arrangements to take your college entrance exams-ACT or SAT. You'll need some money to take the test. Check with your counselor and see how much it costs so you will be prepared.
3. Set aside some time to talk college over with your parents. It is important to talk about expense and location.
4. Find out if you are eligible for a scholarship of any kind.
5. Decide what you are personally looking for in a college and make a list of your requirements.

   For example:

   a. Do you plan to get a degree in a specialty field such as journalism, computer science, or medicine?

   b. Are you interested in spending time in a new city?

   c. Do you plan to compete in a sport?

Dorm Room Cures

When you are in college, your dorm room may not have a lot of space to work with. The goal is to make it as harmonious as possible. Here are some basic rules to follow:

1. When you first move in, open all the windows and let the air circulate and cleanse the room. If you want to get rid of old energy, spray lemon mist in the air or burn sage.

   Here is how to burn sage: Use an old metal baking pan to set the sage in and just light the tip of the sage and gently walk around the room. When you are finished, run the leftover ashes under water to make sure they are not still burning.

2. Get creative with storage. We talked about how important it is to have a clutter free environment, so think about solutions. Try using some see-through bins to organize your things. They are very functional when they are stacked in a closet.

3. Avoid shoving extra stuff under your bed. It is not good to have a lot of clutter blocking the positive flow of chi. If you have to use this space, make sure you have things stored in a neat and orderly fashion. You can use storage bins under your bed but do so sparingly.

4. Don't forget to watch the empty corners of the room. Put a small shelf in a corner to create a circular flow of chi and to give you extra storage!

5. Be alert to sharp corners. Soften the corners by placing an object in front of the sharp edge. For example, if the corner of your desk is pointing right at your body when you sleep, move an object in front of the corner to buffer the edge. A piece of fabric is a good idea. Other corners could use a softened plant or other rounded objects.

6. When you choose artwork for your walls, be careful to choose things that make you feel balanced when you see them and that are not hard on the eyes. Balance the artwork as you do your assessment of elements.

7. If you have a television in your room, try not to make it the focal point. You can have it off to the side or cover it when you are not using it. The bedroom is designed to be an area for peace and tranquility.

CHAPTER FIVE:

Applying Feng Shui to Different Areas in Your Life

Your Automobile

It is important to take a look at all of the areas you come into contact with on a day-to-day basis. Your car is definitely an area that you need to look at because of the amount of time you probably spend driving from one location to another.

Cars are considered extensions of our bodies and should have regular maintenance and upkeep. You want to make sure the effect it has on you and on your passengers is positive. Have you ever ridden in the car with someone and before you even open the door they , say, "Sorry about how messy my car is. Just throw those things in the backseat." Even before you have gotten into the person's car, the situation has produced negative energy. Things that create negative energy in your car are old bags of fast food, gym 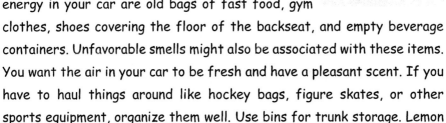 clothes, shoes covering the floor of the backseat, and empty beverage containers. Unfavorable smells might also be associated with these items. You want the air in your car to be fresh and have a pleasant scent. If you have to haul things around like hockey bags, figure skates, or other sports equipment, organize them well. Use bins for trunk storage. Lemon mist can be used to get rid of stale odors and to cleanse the air in your car.

Organizing Your Trunk

Selecting your storage containers is very important. The colors and type will help promote harmony. Select large, hard-plastic bins that fit nicely against one another. With this type of closely packed trunk, you will avoid hearing a lot of noise from crates shifting back and forth. You can also select inexpensive crates that are attractive. Discount hardware stores and general merchandise stores are great places to check out. In addition, you can select wire baskets, braided baskets, wood crates, or milk crates. Make an attempt to organize your trunk into an attractive storage area. You spend a great deal of time in your car and it should reflect organization, symmetry, and attractiveness.

Colors are also important. For harmony on the road, it is important to choose colors that promote relaxation and concentration. In the trunk, for example, you can choose blues, grays, creams, and greens for optimum concentration. If you really want to be organized, you can label your crates appropriately and try to keep the correct items in the labeled crates. Again, it is important to keep your trunk clean, swept, and reorganized from time to time.

When you are cleaning the interior of your trunk, throw away anything that is not a necessity. Always have a place to store your emergency kit, flashlight, and extra blanket. Use the storage crate to store these emergency supplies in your trunk. Another important use of the trunk is storage of sports equipment. Make sure that you have a large enough bin to accommodate the size of the equipment so it can be protected from damage. You can also keep an extra canvas bag for dirty uniforms and equipment so you can keep your trunk smelling nice. Transfer your dirty uniforms or workout clothes immediately to your house or apartment and launder them as soon as possible. Scent is an important factor in positive Feng Shui.

Along with keeping the interior of your car and trunk organized and smelling nice, you need to care for your car in other ways. The time you spend doing regular maintenance, checking your tires, and doing appropriate cleaning will pay off for you many times over in terms of safety and harmony on the road. Having your car working well mechanically can do a lot for increasing the harmony in your life; if you don't have that, it can be very draining on your emotional and physical resources. So, spend half a day at least once a month getting your car in shape. Use this checklist:

Mechanical Checklist
1. Schedule regular oil change (every 3,000 miles).   _____
2. Check windshield wiper blades.   _____
3. Check air in tires.   _____
4. Check any irregular sounds.   _____

Interior/Exterior Checklist
1. Remove clutter/old items.   _____
2. Clean headlights/taillights.   _____
3. Clean and repair windshield.   _____
4. Empty and clean ashtray.   _____
5. Clean dashboard and side panels.   _____
6. Place an emergency kit in trunk (with car jack).   _____
7. Keep a blanket in trunk for emergencies.   _____
8. Always keep extra water and some food supplies. _____

Weekend Activity

Get a group of friends together and detail your cars! Here are the supplies you will need:

1. Old rags
2. Window cleaner
3. Interior cleaner
4. Vacuum with attachment
5. Trash bags
6. Storage crates and other containers for the trunk
7. Car polish for the exterior and interior

Spend some time on getting the exterior of your car in tip-top shape. Work on making the windows clear, which will improve your visibility, especially at night. Use hand towels to get the water spots off the outside of the car and then follow up with a light waxing. After you are finished, notice how you feel when you get into your car. Try to set aside time monthly to keep your car in the best possible shape; it will last longer.

Your Study Space

It is very important to create a separate area to study where you can concentrate. Set yourself up for success by having all the supplies you need organized and in one place. Nothing can be more frustrating and time-consuming than having to go look for missing pens or paper all over the house. Also, make sure you keep the front of your desk clean so you will not block your luck. If you have a lot of stuff piled in front of you, it will represent all the things you have to do. The feeling can be overwhelming. According to Feng Shui principles, it is ideal to have your study area (or office) apart from where you sleep because your bedroom is supposed to be for rest. However, because of space issues, and having one room to work with, you can try to keep your desk as far away from the bed as possible. You can even put in a simple screen to divide the space.

When you are deciding where to move your desk, try to place it where you can see the door when you are sitting in the desk chair. Feng Shui practitioners believe when your back is facing the door you may feel uneasy and want to turn around to see if anyone has entered the room. This situation can be very disruptive and you might have trouble concentrating.

Even if you have to pull the desk out and sit behind it, you are at least in a better position than facing the wall. Try putting your desk where you will face one of your positive directions as well.

Hannah, a teenager from Wisconsin, had this unique challenge with her desk. She had her desk facing a wall so her back was facing the door to her room. When asked if she had trouble concentrating when she studied, she said she had a hard time staying focused. She said she felt uneasy and wanted to look over her shoulder every few minutes to see if anyone had come in her room. The solution was to move her desk facing north (to one of her good directions) so she could see the door when she sat in the desk. Hannah could also do the following to achieve the same effect:

1. The desk can be moved so that Hannah is seated behind it and looking toward the door.

2. The desk can be moved to one of the side walls and Hannah would be seated facing the desk so she could look to her right at the door.

Not only are colors important in your locker and car, they are extremely important in your study area. The colors you choose can help you focus, read, and learn or keep you from concentrating and learning. There have been many psychological studies regarding color, and we now know a great deal about the colors to choose for different environments. For example, pink was found to be very soothing in prisons, so many prisons were painted pink. Blue was found to be very soothing but not very appropriate for the appetite, so many restaurants avoid the color blue. In your study area, the colors found most important for enhancing study are light blue, green, and neutrals. Patterns should be avoided because they can be disruptive. Loud colors like red, for example, should be avoided because red has been found to cause stress and anxiety. Also, avoid the darker colors like navy, purple, and black. These colors also limit your focus and concentration. Look around your study area and see what you can do to bring the soothing, relaxing colors of green and blue to that area. Notice the immediate difference when you start to read, work a math problem, or write a term paper.

Remember, if you create an environment that gives you comfort, you will have an easier time accomplishing your goals. It is very important that you have an easy way to look at the door to see who is coming in. Look around your place of study or any other rooms and make sure that you have followed this guideline!

Here are some tips to remember with regard to your study area:

* Take inventory of what supplies you are missing like pens, scissors, tape, markers, etc. and restock. Place these supplies in attractive, neat containers.

* Get an expandable filing box to store important papers like report cards, job applications, etc.

* If you don't have good lighting, get a desk lamp so you can see what you are doing.

* Make sure you are seated in the correct position in relationship to the door. You must be able to see who is coming in quite easily. Avoid having your back to the door.

Study area checklist:

1. Do you sit facing one of your four good directions? _____
2. Can you see the door from this position? _____
3. Do you have pens, pencils, and highlighters? _____
4. Do you have scissors, tape, paper clips, and a stapler? _____
5. Is there a file box to store important papers? _____
6. Are your supplies organized and easy to reach? _____
7. Is the area well lit? _____
8. Are the corners of the desk rounded with an object? _____
9. Do the colors around you allow you to concentrate? _____
10. Is the front of your desk free of clutter? _____
11. Are your storage containers attractive and the correct colors for studying and concentrating? _____

"The average American will spend one year searching through desk clutter looking for misplaced objects."
—Margin, Dr. Richard Swenson

Organizing For Success

One of the basic components of Feng Shui is organization. Purchase a calendar or day planner so you can keep track of important test dates and deadlines so you are not taken off guard. Inexpensive planners are sold at office supply stores.

A month-at-a-glance planner is nice because you can see what is coming up socially or academically. Include things like your exercise program or job hours so everything is written down in one place. If you have a test coming up, write the date of the test on the calendar. Then work backwards and block out the time you need to study in your planner before the test so that you are prepared. Have some notepaper in your planner to write down spontaneous notes so you don't just scribble on the border.

If you start to use these basic organization ideas, you will feel less stress because you will be more in control of your life. Use the calendar in your planner to start mapping out activities and events that are coming up. You can transfer your goals from the Goal-Setting Exercise you completed earlier in the book.

Fun Activity: Make Your Own Day Planner
Supplies:
Plain typing paper
Hole punch
Hole reinforcements
Notebook
Highlighters
Markers

Current calendar

Ruler

Directions:

1. Using your ruler, draw the grid lines for your weeks and days for that particular month. Leave yourself enough room to write in the squares. Think about having the calendar cover two pages so when you open up that month, you can write more detail.

2. Number the squares on your grid to match the correct day of the month.

3. Hole-punch the sides of your calendar to fit in the notebook. Make sure if your calendar covers two pages that the two pages face together, and then punch the holes in the sides.

4. Write down all academic and social events. Use your highlighters or markers to add color and emphasize important dates.

5. Use fabric or shelf paper to cover the outside of your day planner.

Your new planner is done! Enjoy not having the stress of not knowing what is coming up.

There is an activity and goals section at the end of your calendar sample. Here are some ideas you can write in that section:

Goals:

Example: To study fifteen minutes a day for my history exam

Example: To sign up for the basketball team by Wednesday

Activities:

Examples: To make Valentine cookies with my friends

Examples: To meet my running group every morning at 6:00 for a mile run.

If you have a computer, you can run your own calendars from the web or from Microsoft Word or Publisher.

January

Sunday	Monday	Tuesday	Wednesday	Thursday	Friday	Saturday

Goals and Activities:

1._____
2._____
3._____
4._____
5._____
6._____
7._____

February

Sunday	Monday	Tuesday	Wednesday	Thursday	Friday	Saturday

Goals and Activities:

1._____
2._____
3._____
4._____
5._____
6._____
7._____

March

Sunday	Monday	Tuesday	Wednesday	Thursday	Friday	Saturday

Goals and Activities:

1._____
2._____
3._____
4._____
5._____
6._____
7._____

April

Sunday	Monday	Tuesday	Wednesday	Thursday	Friday	Saturday

Goals and Activities:

1._____
2._____
3._____
4._____
5._____
6._____
7._____

May

Sunday	Monday	Tuesday	Wednesday	Thursday	Friday	Saturday

Goals and Activities:

1._____
2._____
3._____
4._____
5._____
6._____
7._____

June

Sunday	Monday	Tuesday	Wednesday	Thursday	Friday	Saturday

Goals and Activities:

1._____

2._____

3._____

4._____

5._____

6._____

7._____

Also, if you don't already have one, think about getting a backpack or a bag with compartments so you can easily transport your stuff from home to school in an organized way.

Your Backpack

Having one central place to store your books and school supplies is a great idea. When you are going from one class to another and from home back to school, it helps to have a way to keep all of your things orderly. Look for a bag or backpack that has a main compartment for books and several side compartments to store highlighters, pens and pencils. It is also a bonus to have a place to store water and a snack if you will be studying away from home for a long period of time.

Water clears the brain, so keep yourself hydrated by drinking water all day long. You need to carry a bottle with you at all times. Most of us need a minimum of eight glasses of water a day.

As you look at the backpack here, think about how you can arrange it so that it helps you stay organized and calm. Remember to place your water bottles in a secure place so that they don't leak.

Another important thing to remember is to make time to eat healthy. Try to grab healthy snacks along the way to eat between meals to sustain your energy. Again, set yourself up for success by storing some extra granola bars in your backpack so you are prepared.

Your Locker

The locker, like all of your spaces, is just as important to organize. Look at your locker and fig-  ure out what containers to put your things in so that it is organized. For example, you can place your books on a mini-shelf on the floor of the locker. Papers can be placed at the top on cardboard containers to store each folder. Girls can have a container for purse, cosmetics, and personal items. Guys can have containers for sports equipment, keys, and extra hats and clothing. You can also put pictures in your locker to remind you of loved ones or just to inspire you. Remember to place your pictures in the locker in an attractive way. Try to stay away from placing them in a crooked fashion, makeshift and dog-eared! Just keep design in mind and take some time to organize your locker. It can be an attractive place, just like all your other areas. It can reflect you in a positive way!

Developing A Healthy Relationship With Your Parents

In Feng Shui everything ties together. When you start making positive changes in your own environment, good things will spill over into other areas of your life. Look at the people you interact with on a daily basis, like your parents, and try to plan some activities together. As teenagers, it is certainly important for you to be independent and to spend time with your friends. Remember the importance of balance. It is also important to create positive energy with your family, and that means spending some regular time with them if possible. Share the ideas you have learned so far. Feng Shui principles can be applied to any room they have. Get your parents involved in some of the activities mentioned in this workbook; it can be a lot of fun! Family members may want to try some of these ideas themselves.

Garage or Yard Sale

This is a great family project because everyone can be involved. Here are the basic supplies you will need:

1. Poster board for signs
2. Sticky tags to price items
3. Tables for display
4. Balloons for sign
5. Cash box to make change

The first step is to go from room to room in the house and decide what items are worth keeping and what items should be sold. It is important to be very objective. Use this rule: If you have not used the item in two years then sell it or give it to a thrift store. Designate a spot just for garage sale items (the basement is usually a great option) and neatly display each thing that will need to be priced.

The second step is to find extra tables that can be used to display what is being sold. Store these tables neatly in the basement or in whatever area you have chosen as the "garage sale" area.

Next, clean the garage. Take some time to sweep the floor and to get the garage looking great. Here are some tips that might help:

• Hang shovels and brooms on the side of the garage.
• Wrap extension cords and store on a shelf or hang them from a large nail.

- Store sports equipment in large bins.
- Move all related items together.
    -Gardening supplies
    -Paint supplies
    -Tools
    -Camping equipment
- Put miscellaneous items in boxes and label with a marker.

Finally, use sticky tags to price all of your items and arrange them attractively on the tables. It is a good idea to put the price tags on a legal pad after each one is sold so you can track how much money you have made. The balloons are a nice touch and might catch the eye of someone who was unaware of the sale.

Think about taking all the items that did not sell to a thrift store. This is a great way to create good karma. Have fun!

House Repair

Another family project is to make a list of everything that needs to be repaired around the house. Make a schedule of when you can get each thing done and assign tasks to all family members. It is important to remember that not everything needs to be done all at once. That could be an overwhelming task! Instead, think about projects that can be done monthly. It is an important rule of Feng Shui that everything be in working order. Things that don't work or that are broken can be a drain on everyone's energy. This rule is very important, so please take this seriously in your planning. It doesn't have to cost a lot to make the repairs, but they need to be done.

House Repair Schedule

Repairs Needed	Goal Date:	Date Completed:

Here are some other great ideas to do together:

• Make a trip to the local Goodwill together to haul away the extra stuff that you no longer use. You might find some old winter coats in the hall closet that someone can use this winter. Great karma!

Accomplished _____

• Make sure you have an even amount of Yin (dark) and Yang light) in the living room. Make a list of all the light and dark items and make sure they are present in equal amounts. Do this just as you did for your bedroom.

Accomplished _____

• Survey the kitchen together and make sure your stove area is clean, because it is symbolic of good fortune and should not be dirty. Make sure you have plenty of spices and oils, at a safe distance from the heating elements, around the cooking area because this creates the image of great abundance.

Accomplished _____

• Go on a family hike to enjoy nature and get a fresh perspective. Take an afternoon away to share ideas for the future.

Accomplished _____

Building Friendships

As you start making positive changes in your environment, you want to also take a look at the outside influences that affect you on a daily basis. Friends may spend as much time interacting with and influencing you as your parents. As you study Feng Shui, you will begin to realize that the people you hang out with are extremely important. Think about your friends for a minute. You are going to have to analyze them carefully in terms of the kind of energy they emit. You will feel really great and positive when you hang out with upbeat, friendly, goal-oriented people. You will begin to feel down, discouraged, and hurt if you continue to hang out with people who are negative, bitter, and critical. Critical friends, in particular, bring negative energy to people because they are always looking at you in a critical, negative way. When is the last time that person gave you a compliment or an encouraging word? You might not remember even one time when that happened. It is difficult to remove yourself from people like this because often they are manipulative and fulfill a need that you have. But try to distance yourself from those people and not let them into your intimate space. You can still be friendly and warm to them, but you won't hang out with them as much.

Let's think about space for a minute. Following is a diagram that will help you think about space.

 Space Empathy

Intimate Space   (I)

Personal Space   (P)

Social Space   (S)

Public Space   (P)

Here is a short lesson in current psychology for you to think about. This idea is contained in Stephen Nowicki's book, *How to Help the Child Who Doesn't Fit In*. Dr. Nowicki talks about the importance of keeping certain boundaries. His idea fits in very well with the notion of Feng Shui. As you have learned, putting things in containers, organizing your physical space, and creating harmonious pathways will help you in your whole life. Friendships and acquaintanceships are the same way. They need to be put in certain boundaries for your life to become harmonious and prosperous. Try these ideas and see for yourself!

1). Intimate Space. This space is for people you really trust. These individuals are people you can hug and confide in. There are VERY FEW people who have earned the right to be in your intimate space.

2). Personal Space. This is the space around you about three feet out. Think of a hula hoop, and you will feel comfortable with these types of people in your personal space: friends (not the best ones), people you work with, some family members, and students and teachers.

3). Social Space. This space is about five feet around you. People fitting in that space includes employers, neighbors, people you just met, lecturers, and people you aren't sure of.

4). Public Space. This space is ten feet around you. These people are ex-boyfriends or girlfriends (most of the time!), public speakers, performers, and complete strangers.

The importance of using this target in your everyday life is to help you understand that not everyone goes in your intimate space. They have to earn that honor! So try standing in the appropriate space when you are dealing with people and you will be amazed at the results. For example, try standing five feet away from a potential employer when you are applying for a job. Pity the poor person who stands in the employer's intimate space! Their application will have a good chance of ending up in the round file (the wastebasket.) Try this. It works!

Now, take a long hard look at your current friends. How do they treat other people? Do they encourage you to grow as a person and accomplish your goals? Are they positive people who plan to have a bright future? If you do not like your answers, think about making some changes. Start to gradually do activities with new people who have the same interests you do. Cherish the friends who are worth having and keep the others as acquaintances. Gravitate toward people who complement your personality and whom you truly have a great time around. You should start to feel happier and healthier as a person because of these positive new relationships.

Take a few minutes to assess your friends:

Friend #1:_____		Friend #2:_____	
Quality	**Yes/No**	**Quality**	**Yes/No**
Trustworthy	_____	Trustworthy	_____
Caring	_____	Caring	_____
Good listener	_____	Good listener	_____
Goal-oriented	_____	Goal-oriented	_____
Positive attitude	_____	Positive attitude	_____
Fun	_____	Fun	_____

Friend #3:_____   Friend #4:_____

Quality	Yes/No	Quality	Yes/No
Trustworthy	_____	Trustworthy	_____
Caring	_____	Caring	_____
Good listener	_____	Good listener	_____
Goal-oriented	_____	Goal-oriented	_____
Positive attitude	_____	Positive attitude	_____
Fun	_____	Fun	_____

Summarize your friendships here:

My friends are generally_____

_____

Am I happy with my friends?

_____

My friendships need to change? _____

My goal is _____

Potential Friends and Numbers of Contacts

Name	Contact 1	Contact 2	Contact 3	Contact 4

Activities with New Friends

Name	Activity 1	Activity 2	Activity 3	Activity 4

If you want to connect with new friends and place yourself in positive situations, then participate in activities with people who radiate positive energy. Avoid activities where people are emitting negative energy. Examples include:

1. Sports or fitness groups
2. Foreign language clubs
3. Charity work
4. Book clubs
5. Yoga classes
6. Cooking classes
7. Chess clubs
8. YMCA groups
9. Acting groups
10. Ceramics classes
11. Writing clubs
12. Hiking groups

13. Church groups for teens

14. Computer classes or clubs

Your high school counseling and guidance department usually has a list of neat groups in your particular area. The counselor can also administer a test to find out what your interests are and can help guide you to an appropriate group. Remember, try to hang out with other people who are setting goals and trying to achieve in a positive way. Being around those people will be a great boost to you and your self-esteem.

Write some potential clubs in this "future cloud" and take steps to join right away. You will be glad you did!

Relationships with a Significant Other

Apply the same rules that you would for choosing friends to choosing a person to have a relationship with. Does this person encourage you to grow as a person and accomplish your goals? Is he or she a positive person who wants to have a bright future? Do you really enjoy spending time with this person? If you answer no to any of these questions, consider moving on. It seems like people attract the same type of person based on what they are projecting out into the world. Healthy people with interesting things going on in their lives usually attract people with those same qualities.

Also, make sure you have taken care of balancing your own life before trying to juggle a relationship. For example, if you are struggling academically, come up with a plan of action to correct your situation. Then you might want to introduce another person into your life.

You might want to get to know people as friends first. Watch how they react in different situations; this is a great way to find out if you even want to take the relationship further. Invite them to a prom or homecoming as a friend and see what happens.

It is important to be selective about the people you surround yourself with because it can determine the quality of life you create for yourself.

Also, take a minute to assess your boyfriend or girlfriend. Think about what you've learned and set a goal. You might only have to set a goal to maintain a wonderful relationship, or you might want to change or leave a negative relationship.

Name of boyfriend or girlfriend _____

Qualities	Yes	No
Trustworthy	_____	_____
Fun-loving	_____	_____
Good heart	_____	_____
Unselfish	_____	_____
Good listener	_____	_____
Goal-oriented	_____	_____
Enjoys family	_____	_____

****

Name of friend _____

Qualities	Yes	No
Trustworthy	_____	_____
Fun-loving	_____	_____
Good heart	_____	_____
Unselfish	_____	_____
Good listener	_____	_____
Goal-oriented	_____	_____
Enjoys family	_____	_____

****

Name of friend _____

Qualities	Yes	No
Trustworthy	_____	_____

Fun-loving   _____   _____
Good heart   _____   _____
Unselfish   _____   _____
Good listener   _____   _____
Goal-oriented   _____   _____
Enjoys family   _____   _____

It is very important be a giving person in a relationship, whether it is with your significant other or with a family member or a friend. One of the main principles of Feng Shui is that if you are a giving person in a relationship, then you will receive that much more. If you find out that you are giving, however, and the other person is not, then you need to pull back and consider removing yourself from the relationship.

By "giving", we don't mean physically or sexual giving; we mean showing consideration and concern in the following ways.

1) **Empathy.** One of the most important things you can do to establish a good relationship is to really listen and listen in a serious way. Empathy means not interrupting, not telling your own story, and not being critical when someone tells you something. Key elements in listening are holding your body in a listening way, using soft eyes as you look at the person, being able to assess the correct feeling in someone, responding appropriately with your face and being able to summarize what the person said and how they are feeling.

2) **Supportive of Goals.** Supporting your friends as they establish positive goals is very important. You have to be discerning here, though. Sometimes your friends might set destructive goals, like being in a gang, for example, or shoplifting from a store or doing drugs. You have to be supportive of the person but tell the person

honestly that you will be supportive of positive goals. These goals would include achieving well in school or sports, maintaining a job, helping the family, and participating in volunteer activities.

3) **Simple Gestures.** There are many things you can do in relationships that don't take very much time but are very important in building that relationship. Notes to your friend are wonderful ways to communicate that you care. Bringing a small gift occasionally or making a gift shows that you care. Sending a card or e-mail that is supportive is great. Taking the time to compliment your friend or to give words of encouragement really is helpful. Remember to think about the person and what would really be helpful to him or her. Then take the time to do it.

4) **Positive Reinforcement.** As we said in the previous paragraph, positive reinforcement is very important. This is shown by notes, comments, e-mails, and or cards that show the person you have noticed something good that was done. If your friend baked you a cake for your birthday, then tell the person how great that was and how happy and appreciated it made you feel. When your boyfriend writes you a great note, tell him how much you appreciated his taking the time to do that. When your friend gives you flowers, take the time to say thank you! You will find that people do a lot more for you when you focus on the positive.

Take a couple of minutes to think about how you are doing in the area of friendship. Let's do a self-evaluation activity and then set a goal that will help us enrich our friendships. These actions can really bring harmony and abundance into our lives. Complete the following chart and then let's set a friendship goal!

My Friendship Self-Assessment

Friends	Empathy	Supportive of Goals	Simple Gestures	Positive Reinforcement
1.				
2.				
3.				
4.				
5.				
6.				

Now, as you have looked at yourself related to the "giving" factor, it is time to set some goals for yourself—in terms of friendship.

Goal-Setting Exercise #2

Set a goal that you can achieve within the next two weeks regarding your friends or significant other. Write that goal here:

I will _____.

Check to make sure that your goal meets the criteria for effective goal-setting.

1. Is my goal realistic?_____

2. Do I want to do this?_____

3. Is the goal written in a positive way?_____

4. Can I measure my goal easily?_____

How can you use positive self-talk to help you achieve your goal?
I can say _____ to myself.

Can you do any thing else to help yourself achieve your goal?
Write your ideas here _____

_____

How did I do on this goal?

Not that great _____   Okay   _____

Good job   _____   Super job   _____

Finding Personal Time

Personal time is very important for balance in your life. You can use this time to reconnect with yourself by doing yoga, reading a novel, painting, hiking, building things, or any activity you enjoy doing away from other people. If it means blocking out some time in your planner and calling it "me time," then do it.

A great way to see if you are over committed is to write down everything you do for two weeks. Track your activities daily by blocking the time out on a monthly or weekly calendar. You can use the calendar in this book under "Organizing for Success". At the end of the two weeks, evaluate how you are spending your time. You might be surprised!

Remember to set realistic goals and not be committed to so many activities that you don't have time to relax. Give yourself the luxury to make time for the things you love to do. Listen to your body. If you are starting to feel run-down or overwhelmed, slow down.

An example of a typical day might look like this:

7:45-11:30	Classes
12:00	Run two-miles/grab lunch
1:30-3:00	Classes
3:15-4:30	Meet study group
5:30-6:30	Dinner
7:00-8:30	Work on project for art class

A day like this seems as if it could be hard to schedule any personal time. Even if you reserved 8:30 to 9:30 for reading your favorite book, do not let phone calls from friends interrupt your time. Even though getting phone calls is exciting, sometimes it is nice to have some time to yourself. When you block out time with yourself to do something you love, you will feel more balanced and fulfilled with your lifestyle.

It is a good idea to keep a record of how much personal time you are allowing yourself. Here is a page from a personal time journal that you can copy and put in your own three-ring binder. Record for a month!

My Personal Time Record

Week _____

Date	Activity	Activity	Activity	Activity	Activity
Mon					
Tues					
Wed					
Thurs					
Fri					
Sat					
Sun					

Now assess your amount of leisure time:

* Just the right amount   _____
* I need more time   _____
* I need less time   _____

Set a goal to increase or decrease your leisure time.

Yoga and Breathing

When we talk about yoga, we are not talking about any religious move-ment; we are talking about the stretching and breathing exercises that yoga practice has to offer. Many research studies show that practicing the breathing and stretching of yoga can really help you bring harmony into your life. Again, we suggest that you try some of these and see for yourself.

When we show you these exercises, remember that the most impor-tant thing is to take deep, long breaths during each stretch. There is something about breathing into the stretch that helps loosen your mus-cles, increase flexibility, and expand your lungs.

Start with practicing the three-part breath. Once you get accustomed to doing this breath, practice it several times a day. And for those who participate in sports, this is very useful prior to games or practice.

Three-Part Breath

1. Start to inhale deep within your LOWER abdomen through your nose.
2. Continue lifting your breath up through your stomach.
3. Now give that extra lift to the breath and bring the air all the way to your upper lunch.
4. Exhale in order of breathing in...lungs, stomach, then abdomen.

Centering Posture

1. Stand with your feet about a foot apart.
2. Shift your body gently from side to side and land softly in the middle.
3. Now rock your body gently backward and forward and land in the middle.
4. Firmly inhale into your three-part breath, tucking in your stomach and your back side.
5. Exhale, but leave some tension in your upper thighs.
6. Relax your shoulders and feel the wonderful balance!

Side Bend

1. Stand in your centering posture.
2. Inhale bringing both arms up over your head with your palms facing each other.
3. Slowly bend to your right, holding the posture for a few seconds as you breathe.
4. Slowly come upright again.
5. Gently bend over to the left, remembering to breathe into the stretch.
6. Inhale up to your standing position and drop your arms.

Back Side Stretch

1. Lie down on your back where you have plenty of room.
2. Lift your left leg up and wrap your arms around it.
3. Slowly move your left leg across your body and bend it to the floor on your right. Hold and breathe.
4. Bring your left leg back and gently put it on the floor.
5. Inhale bringing your right leg up, and grab it with your arms.
6. Slowly move your right leg across to the left and get it close to the floor if you can. Breathe.
7. Bring your right leg back and place it on the floor.

Rocking on Your Back.

1. While lying on your back, lift both legs up and grab each knee with the appropriate hand—right hand grabs right knee and left hand grabs left knee.
2. Slowly rock back and forth from left to right.
3. Breathe deeply as you rock and feel the stretch on your spine.
4. Slowly bring your legs back into position on the floor.

Forward Bend

1. While sitting on the floor, bring your legs together and your arms to your sides.
2. Inhale, bringing your arms up and over your head with your hands clasped together.
3. Bring your feet gently toward you and remain in that position.
4. Slowly inhale, then while exhaling, bend your body gently toward your feet. (Don't push too hard—your body will stretch in time!)
5. Breathe in that position for a few seconds, gently bring your arms back over your head, then down to your sides.

Warrior

1. Stand in the centering position.
2. Inhale, bringing your arms up over your head.
3. Step forward with your right foot and bend the knee.
4. Straighten your back leg and breathe.
5. You can also place your arms forward, as shown in the drawings, or onto your knee.
6. Then switch feet. It is important to do both sides!

Standing Forward Stretch

1. Stand in your centering position.
2. Inhale, bringing your arms up over your head, with your palms facing out toward the room.
3. Exhale gently, bending over very gently from your spine until you can dangle your arms in the forward position.
4. Rock slowly from side to side, feeling your spine loosen.

The Lunge

This stretch is wonderful for the upper thigh.
Again, go easy when you start.
1. Stand in the centering position with your legs
   wide apart.
2. Inhale, bringing your arms up even with your shoulders.
3. Step to your right and bend the right knee.
4. Bring your arms slowly down to the floor for balance.
5. Breathe.
6. Lift your arms again to your sides.
7. Bring your leg back to center.
8. Repeat on the left side.

The Squat

This stretch is great for strength and stamina building. Start with a
short squat, then try to increase your time to a minute or two.
1. Inhale, bringing your arms up over your head.
2. Exhale, bringing your arms to the front of your body.
3. Bring your body to a partial squatting position.
4. Breathe into the stretch.
5. Try to hold the stretch increasingly for longer periods.

The Cobra

The Cobra is great for stretching the back, but go very easy when you start.

1. Lie down on your stomach with your face turned to the side on the floor.
2. Place your arms by your side with palms on the floor.
3. Gently move your hands close to your sides just below your shoulder about halfway down toward your waist.
4. Inhale, raising your upper body just a little at first, and breathe. Your face should be looking up as illustrated in the drawing.

The Bow

The bow is a nice stretch for your legs and back. Do this gradually, a little at a time.

1. Lie down on your stomach, your hands at your sides, palms down.
2. Inhale and reach back to your ankles, grabbing them gently.
3. Exhale, lifting your legs up gradually with your arms.
4. Breathe into the stretch, lifting your head up.
5. Gently place your legs back on the floor, releasing your hands.
6. Keep breathing for a couple of seconds with your head at your side.

The Tree Pose

This stretch is wonderful for balancing.
1. Place your feet about six inches to one foot apart.
2. Inhale, bringing your arms up over your head.
3. Bring your palms together.
4. Relax your shoulders.
5. Breathe into the stretch.

Note: If you have health problems or have a back or other injury, please consult your physician before doing these exercises. If you have any questions, call your local yoga or fitness center and sign up for a class where the instructor can work with you on appropriate postures. Remember, go into these postures very gently until your body begins to respond. This is not like calisthenics where you are jumping, pushing, and pressing yoga has to do with stretching your body while breathing.

Finding the Right Clothes

Finding clothes that make you feel confident and reflect who you are is important. When you are building your wardrobe, take a long hard look at what you already have. Having an excess of clothes you never wear is a Feng Shui negative. If you have worked through the Declutter Exercise in chapter two, you are ahead of the game!

Stand outside of your closet and look in. Try to arrange everything so you can see it. You will be surprised how many outfits you can put together from what you already have. Get some clear, plastic, stackable crates so you can organize accessories. When you keep adding items, they will be visible at all times.

It is good to get ideas from magazines, but make sure to add your own personal flair. Keep only the clothes that make you feel good and are comfortable to wear. Be sure to ask your friends' opinions because they will most certainly tell you.

Here are some inexpensive ways to start building your wardrobe:

1. Order some catalogues and fashion magazines from your favorite store and determine which parts of the outfits you like.

2. Get a group of your friends together and have a clothes-swapping party. Bring items that you have not worn because maybe the color was wrong but might look great on someone else.

3. When you drop off clothes at the thrift store, take a quick peek around to see if you can find anything you like.

4. Consider having a garage sale in the neighborhood and encourage families to participate.

5. Regularly shop at surplus stores and discount shops. You will be able to grab the best bargains if you are a regular customer.

6. You and your friends might want to take in a local fashion show at the mall to see what new fashions are emerging this next season.

Storage Tips

After you purchase clothes, it is important to store them correctly using Feng Shui principles. Your things need to be organized well so that you are able to see at a glance exactly what you have. It is a good idea to organize your clothing by type and color first. Then it would help if you would organize your clothes by season. By taking the time to organize up front, it will save you much time in the long run.

If you have trouble getting rid of things, every time you wear something, turn the hanger backwards and then give yourself six months. If you haven't worn the item in that period of time, think about giving it away to a thrift store, a neighbor, or a friend. It is important that you remove items that you no longer wear.

Your drawers are just as important as your closet. You should have drawer space for your underwear and socks. A separate drawer can be kept for colored socks and white socks. If you live in a climate that lends itself to lots of winter sports, you will likely have quite a large number of both colored and white socks. They need to be separated into different drawers. T-shirts can have their own drawer. Pants and slacks need to have a separate drawer, and so can shirts. Your nice things, however, should be hung in closet space.

The closet needs to be an attractive space. Keep your space visually appealing. Do this is by first organizing your clothes by type, color, and season. Then purchase hangers of the same style and color. Crates or and other containers can be colorful and of various textures. They are available in discount stores, and inexpensive. Elsewhere in this book, you will find instructions for making your own storage containers using the theme you have selected. For example, if you choose a Monet theme, which is artistic, you will have pinks and greens with pastel containers and hangers. By contrast, if you choose a "Pottery Barn" theme, you will have golds, rusts, browns, and lots of metal. Your closet should be a place that makes you feel good entering to select your clothes and accessories.

If you really think about it, your closet is an area of your room that you will most likely see first thing in the morning. How your clothes and other personal items are arranged can set the tone for your day. Think about the two scenarios below and notice how easily it can happen.

Scenario #1

Isabel woke up at 6:50 and realized that she had not set her alarm! Her ride to school was coming to pick her up at 7:10, and they could not be late because they were to give a group presentation. She jumped out of bed and ran to wash her face and brush her teeth. While she patted her face dry with a towel, she ran to her closet frantically looking for something to wear. She thought her new black pants would be perfect, but she could not find them. She rummaged through some clothes that were heaped in a pile on the floor of her closet. Oops! She had forgotten she had worn them Saturday and they were dirty. She thought about her tan pants, but they would work only with the brown belt. The brown belt was nowhere to be seen. Isabel began to throw things out of the closet, getting more frustrated by the minute. She finally settled on an outfit she did not feel comfortable in so that she could catch her ride.

Scenario #2

Isabel woke up at 6:50 and realized that she had not set her alarm. Her ride to school was coming to pick her up at 7:10, and they could not be late because they were to give a group presentation. She jumped out of bed and ran to wash her face and brush her teeth. While she patted her face dry with a towel, she ran to her closet frantically looking for something to wear. She felt a sigh of relief when she noticed how easily it was to find her clothes. She did not see her black pants hanging in the closet and realized they must be in the dirty clothes. Thinking fast, she grabbed her tan pants and took down the belt box from her closet to locate her brown belt. It was easy to find a shirt to match the outfit because her shirts were lined up in a row at the top of her closet. Isabel threw her outfit on and still had a few extra minutes to put on her makeup and make her ride. She was not thrilled about not having time to shower, but felt happy that she pulled it off with little stress.

Scenario #3

Juan was running late for the bus. He had just remembered that he had soccer practice after school and had to pay his dues for the year. He panicked and ran downstairs to see if he could catch his mom before she left to get a check. He could not find her anywhere. He ran and jumped in the shower, and trying to remember if he had taken his baseball glove out of Josh's car. He ran out of the shower and searched frantically through all of his drawers. He found his shirt crumpled under a wet towel from yesterday and shoved it in his backpack. He had no time to eat breakfast or to call Josh, and he did not have a check to pay for his dues.

Scenario #4

Juan was running late for the bus. He quickly looked at his calendar and remembered that he had soccer practice after school. He remembered that he had already placed his equipment into the equipment container in his car. He took a quick shower and put on the clothes he had laid out last night. After grabbing a cereal bar from the pantry and his drink from the refrigerator, he calmly picked up the check he had reminded his mom to write the night before.

Set yourself up for success so when things do not go as planned you are prepared! Keeping your closet in good order is a plus and a Feng Shui basic. Now let's get creative...

Think of ways to bring your own personal flair into organizing your closet. You are your own designer! First, think of things that can really accent your closet. Here are some ideas:

• Get a rice steamer and use it to store accessories. The different layers of the steamer will separate your items so you can find them easily. Rice steamers come in light brown, but with a little paint you can add some color.

• Use all of the same style of hangers (wood hangers look great and work well for hanging suits).

• Muffin baking tins make great storage for earrings or necklaces. If you are making your own jewelry, the little cups are perfect for keeping beads from rolling and getting lost.

• Store sports uniforms in a separate part of the closet and use one hanger for the shirt and pants.

• Use a beach bag to store summer shoes and hang it on the side of your closet.

• Cover old shoeboxes and use them to store belts and larger accessories. Pick your favorite fabric and glue it to the outside of the box.

Here is a project to cover shoeboxes or baskets to add color to your closet. Grab some friends and try this on a weekend!

Fun Project: Creative Boxes or Baskets

Supplies:
  Box or basket
  Elmer's glue
  Fabric
  Glitter
  Beads
  Paintbrush

Boxes:

1. Find a shoebox that is not being used for anything.

2. Locate some fabric and glue it on the outside of the box.

3. Use a brush to apply glue, you can add a little water to the glue to allow it to easily brush onto the back of the fabric.

4. Let it dry.

Baskets:

1. Find a basket that you can spray-paint.

2. Find some spray paint in a color you like. Spray-paint the basket in a well-ventilated area or a basement with lots of newspaper and an open window.

3. Add glitter or glue beads to the outside of the basket.

Have fun!

Getting a Part-Time Job

A part-time job is a great way to open up new doors while building your work experience. You are exposed to new people and learning while you earn money. This is a way to positively affect your human luck because you can use the money to do something good for yourself. Figure out how many hours you can afford to work without letting other things in your life get out of balance. If an after-school job or weekend job is too much, then plan for the summer. Think about what you would like to do and then start contacting the right people. Think about what kind of person you are and what situations you feel the most comfortable in.

If you are more of a people person, look for a job that involves interacting with people. Examples include coaching a sport, and working as a tutor, clothing store clerk, or lifeguard.

If you are more of an introvert and like dealing with processes rather than with people directly, consider jobs like office assistant, computer entry or working with plants or animals.

Here's how to start:

- Make sure you have figured out how many hours you can work. (Hint: More than twenty is too much while you are in school!)
- Figure out how you will get to and from your place of employment.
- Check around locally for "help wanted" signs.
- Look in the Sunday paper under part-time jobs.

- Ask around and find out if any openings are available in a field in which you might be interested in the future.
- Visit your counselor and ask for job postings. Some schools have job placement counselors who will help you.

Things to Look For in the Job Environment

You can learn to observe your potential job environments to see if they have positive Feng Shui. Observe how the environment is organized, the colors that are used, how clean the place is, how trash is disposed of, the friendliness of the employees, the nature of the supervisors, and other factors. Here is a checklist for you to use in your observations. You can choose your environment, and it will pay off in the long run.

Work Environment Checklist

Feng Shui Factors	Not Great	Okay	Great
1. Do the other workers look happy?			
2. Is the work-place clean and neat?			
3. Would you enjoy spending long hours in this environment?			
4. Do workers have a good amount of space to use?			
5. Is there good use of color?			
6. Is there positive energy?			

The Job Interview

Working with Feng Shui principles can also help you in that important job interview. As a high school or college student, even your part-time jobs are important in your future career. You will be learning how to be productive, usually around other people, and the skills you learn now will be invaluable for your future.

Factors you need to consider include your dress, your use of personal space, your application and resum'e, your attitude and demeanor, and the information you give during the interview.

Dress

What you wear is critical in a job interview. Just as you would organize your closet using space and color, you need to do the same for your person. Wear clothing that is pleasing to the viewer, meaning that your colors should be conservative for the most part. Wearing neutral colors is calming to an employer. Avoid wearing distracting colors or clothing with heavy patterns. You want your potential employer to notice you, not your clothes. Shoes are important as well. Conservative shoes are an important indicator of your professionalism. If you were applying for a construction worker position, you would still wear clean, conservative jeans and a jacket with a collared shirt. Avoid wearing unpressed, dirty clothes to an interview, or anywhere for that matter!

Use of Personal Space

How you use your space in the interview is important. First of all, most employers feel most comfortable if you greet them in social space. You will recall from the section on use of space that certain people are more comfortable with more distance between you and them. Your potential employer is probably one of those people. Employers usually let you know this by having a huge desk between you and them. Walking into the interview, you will know to introduce yourself, shake hands in a firm manner, and sit in social space. That space is at least five feet between you and the employer. ALWAYS utilize that rule in interviews. Imagine the employer who interviews a person who gets in his or her face. The employer will place that file in the discard pile!

If the situation allows, you could always try to sit with your back toward a wall for support. Often this isn't possible because your employer forces you to sit in front of the desk. But look around and see if you can place your back facing the wall, especially in a group interview.

Application and Resume

You are probably getting so good at this by now that you can already visualize an application and resume that has clean space and neat writing. Today, you can scan in an application form and complete it on the computer. That way, the form is completed with a clean font and looks very well put together and organized. You then make sure your application is kept clean and neat (you can use a folder to store it in) and write your resume.

As a teenager, you can stick to a one-page resume. If you search the Internet, you will see that the one-page resume is somewhat out-of-date. If you have worked for a while and have held several jobs, feel free to add a second page. The Internet is a good place to search for current examples of resume's and resume requirements.

Be sure to include in your resume WHAT YOU HAVE ACCOMPLISHED in your work. Avoid just listing your jobs. Make sure you list at least three references at the end and CALL THE REFERENCES for permission to list them BEFORE you place their names on the resume. Make sure you look up their phone numbers and addresses and have them with you when you do your resume and fill out forms.

Attitude and Demeanor

Your attitude in the interview needs to be positive and emit clear energy. Prior to going into an interview, do some stretching and breathing and stand in the centering posture to make sure that you are in a balanced state. You want your interviewer to be comfortable with you. If you go in there uptight, distracted, nervous, or anxious, this will come across immediately to your employer. It is also important to think about what you want to say to the employer and write a few things down.

Not only is it important to be relaxed and centered in the interview, you need to exude warmth and friendliness. The employer wants to hire people who have good human relations skills and who can get along well with other employees. Your interview is not the time to complain about people who have irritated you or about past employers. Come across as relaxed, friendly, and competent!

Information Given During the Interview

Go into the interview prepared. You need to have information about yourself that you can share. This information would include your strengths, goals, past work experiences, volunteer experiences, and experiences at school. You also need to prepare questions for the interviewer. Most interviewers are looking for people who come prepared with questions for them.

You might have a table such as the one below to take with you. Here is an example of what you might include:

Strengths	Good attitude; hard worker
Goals	Top student, work experience
Past Work Experience	Babysitting, tutoring, Walmart
Volunteer Experience	Nursing home volunteer
School Activities	Varsity cheerleader, basketball team, football team, Yearbook staff, thespian, Outward Bound, camp counselor
Grades	3.4 grade-point average
References	Wayne Fields 13 Birnham Columbia, MO 63303 314-440-3276 Dr. Harold Salmon 440 Westminster Denver, CO 80302 303-822-0987 Reverend James Hawkins Lutheran Church of St. Louis 30 Kingshighway St. Louis, MO 63303 314-998-0099

Remember that when you first start looking for a job, any of your volunteer or work experiences can be used, even if you have never held a "real" job.

As you start building positive work relationships, ask your manager to be a reference for you in the future. See the great results when you start to better yourself. It is an upward spiral!

CHAPTER SIX

Building Your Future

Building your future is a culmination of all the things we have talked about up to this point. Try to change just one thing at a time and pretty soon you will have made a big difference in your life. Look at each day as an opportunity to live the kind of life that makes you happy, balanced, and productive. Feng Shui can help set the stage for change and growth in your life, but you are the captain of your own ship and you decide where you are going. Be your own person, set your own goals, and watch your future unfold!

Here is an exercise that will help you pinpoint your goals and get some clarity on your future. Have fun with this exercise and start making your dreams into reality. If you keep them in your head, they will just stay dreams; once they are written down, they become a plan.

Getting a Clear Vision Exercise

People often do all the right things we talked about earlier, but sit back waiting for things to happen. Make sure you're clear on what things in your life you want to have happen.

Here is a fun exercise you can do to give yourself a visual reminder of what you want. You can invite a group of friends over for a pizza or slumber party or you can decide to create on your own.

Supplies:

Glue stick

Pile of magazines (that you don't mind cutting up)

Poster board or great picture frame

Go through the magazines and find pictures that represent your ideal future. Here are some examples:

- UCLA or any college
- A group of volunteers helping kids
- A cheerleader
- A term paper with an "A" on it

If you can't find it, draw it!

Make room to place a picture of yourself looking confident and happy in the center of the collage. You have now successfully created your ideal world at this time in your life. **Hang it somewhere so that it is easy to see.** Every day you will be reminded of where you are going and what you want in your life. If you ever have one of those stressful days when nothing goes right (we all do), you can look up and see all your positive images of the future.

Here is an idea that you can use for your Collage of the Future.

Draw or cut out positive images in each circle around the center of the collage representing you as a successful individual. Then put the picture where you can see it daily. This establishes positive energy for your future. You can also put a type of medicine wheel in your room, on the refrigerator, or in your locker to make your future goals more concrete. Section off the wheel into areas of your goals, cut out or draw images of success, and look at them daily. This is a technique for reminding you of your goals on a consistent basis.

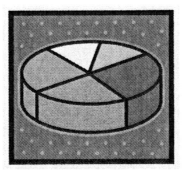

1. Color one section blue. This represents career goals.
2. Color one section green. This represents financial goals.
3. Color one section yellow. This represents learning.
4. Color one section orange. This represents health.
5. Color one section purple. This represents relationships.

My Personal Collage for Success

Place a picture of yourself in the center of the page looking happy and successful.

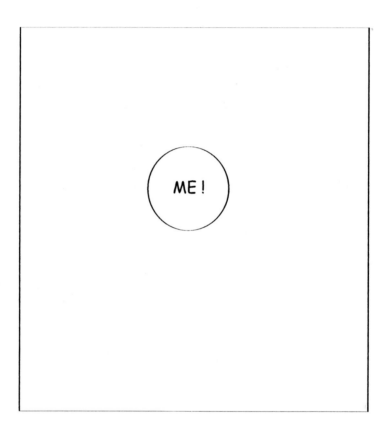

Calendar for Growth and Success

January

Make a fresh start!

1. Get a new planner book for the year.
2. Write down your vision for the year.
3. Establish your goals for both semesters.
4. Think about something positive you want to bring into your life this year
5. Draw a picture of that positive vision in your calendar so that you can see it every day.

February

Remember that what you give to the universe will define the quality of life you lead.

1. Do small random good deeds for friends or family.
2. Make holiday cookies with friends.
3. Send a card to someone who isn't expecting it.
4. Send Valentine cards to everyone you know.
5. Buy your friends some chocolate, or better yet, make some.
6. Write letters and tell people how much you appreciate them.
7. Do a kind deed and don't tell anybody.

March

Practice a breathing exercise each morning.

1. Get some fresh plants to mark the beginning of spring. Make sure the leaves are rounded and that the plants stay healthy.
2. Start a walking or running program in a beautiful, safe place.
3. Give a plant to someone else.
4. Bring a plant to a nursing home and read a story to a patient.

April

Spring is a great time to focus on nature.

1. Start a hiking group.
2. Practice Yoga.
3. Go through your closet and give away things you don't wear.
4. Plant flowers outside and give some seedlings away to your friends and neighbors.
5. Give flowers to people who have been nice to you.

May

May is a wonderful time to do something different. Try something new and positive.

1. Enroll in a new activity for the summer.
2. Add strength training to your exercise regime.

3. Offer to help a family member with a project.

4. Look over your room and create an environment for summer

    a. Add light pillows.

    b. Change the pictures.

    c. Use a soft, light comforter and light sheets.

    d. Use light-colored throw rugs.

    e. Lighten your window treatments.

    f. Do a thorough cleaning.

    g. Spray lemon mist in your room.

June

June is a good time to balance yourself and learn to enjoy the lazy days of summer.

1. Take your journal, sit under a tree and write about your hopes and dreams.
2. Continue your Yoga practice, especially those stretches that are calming and relaxing.
3. Paint or take a ceramics class.
4. Work in a garden, caring for your flowers every day.
5. Write poetry and read it to a friend.

July

Celebrate the Fourth of July with family and friends.

1. Invite friends over for a barbeque.

2. Call someone you don't know and ask them out to lunch.

3. Put the American flag up where everyone can see it.

4. Organize a picnic in a beautiful park.

5. Take a bike ride.

6. Participate in water sports—tubing, waterskiing, boating, snorkeling.

7. Collect rocks and skip them over the water.

August

August is a good time to organize for the year.

1. Make a list of everything you need for the school year.

2. Evaluate your planner and backpack and decide if you need to purchase new ones.

3. Have a car-cleaning party.

4. Analyze your physical body and continue working out so that you are in top physical shape.

5. Work on your Yoga so that you are relaxed and calm and begin to emit positive energy.

September

September is the time of year to go inward and reflect.

1. Look over your goals in your planner and reflect on them. Decide if they are still appropriate.

2. Spend some quiet time just reading a book.

3. Put up a quote that will inspire you to reach your new goals.

4. Go to a football game and drink hot chocolate.

5. Make one new friend.

October

When the leaves are changing, it is a great time to renew your spirit.

1. Look at your room and redecorate it using fall colors.

2. Grab another book and snuggle down and read.

3. Make sure you have a wonderful throw that will keep you warm and cozy.

4. Visit a pumpkin patch and get a few pumpkins for your friends and family.

5. Make a jack-o-lantern and put it on your porch.

6. Have a Halloween party where everyone dresses up in a costume.

November

November is the time to take stock of what you have and to give thanks for your blessings.

1. Help plan and cook a Thanksgiving dinner.

2. Invite someone over who doesn't have a place to go (with your family's permission, of course).

3. Volunteer to work in a soup kitchen.

4. Make a Blessings Book and draw or write something you are thankful for each day.

5. Find out how to donate clothing to families in need.

6. Send out notes and cards of thanks to your friends.

December

December is truly a time of giving and a time to build wonderful memories with friends and family.

1. Try to find out about the childhood of a relative whom you haven't talked with much.
2. Reflect on the past year and choose goals for the new year.
3. Bake holiday cookies from scratch, give some to your family, and give a basket to a nursing home or day care center.
4. Make presents rather than buying them.
5. Reach out and contact someone you haven't seen for a while.
6. Send out a bunch of Christmas cards.
7. Watch _The Christmas Carol_.

Celebrating Success

As you establish your goals and carry them out, you might want to track your progress. Remember, you have your medicine wheel or collage for success out front and open for you to see daily. A daily or weekly journal is a good way for you to celebrate your successes. This doesn't have to be an elaborate or expensive venture. Instead, you can create your own, put it together, and add your own personal touches. If you record your ideas, talk about them, and put them on paper, they are more likely to come true.

So take the time to record your progress in a way that is meaningful to you. This journal will be something you can keep, look back on, and learn from. Making it attractive is another way to practice Feng Shui and bring additional harmony into your life.

Your journal headings could include the date, what occurred, how you felt about what happened, and what you learned about it. You could also include a goal if appropriate. Here is an example of your Celebrating Success Journal, but feel free to design your own!

Success!

Date:

Event:

The Success:

Feelings:

What I'm grateful for and what I'd like to change:

CONCLUSION

This book is designed to help you bring positive energy into your life. You can see how simple it actually is to change your surrounding energy and the energy within yourself.

It takes just a few minutes each day to change your environment. Once you start to do this, you will notice immediate change. You will feel better and have greater control of your life. People will treat you better because they sense the change.

I hope you have learned some great things that will help you transform your environment into an abundant and successful place. These Feng Shui principles can be carried with you and applied to any space you occupy in the future. Stay true to your heart when making your choices in life, and realize there is always room for change. Sometimes these changes in yourself are difficult to make, but you can take one step at a time.

ABOUT THE BOOK

The adolescent years are often a time of confusion and turbulence. One of the ways to deal with the difficulties is to help teenagers use simple Feng Shui techniques to create self-esteem, balance, and success. By learning these techniques, teenagers can help themselves think better, organize better, and make clearer decisions. By changing the bedroom around and adding new and different objects, positive changes are likely to happen. By learning about space boundaries and positive friends, the teenager can transform his or her life and bring in people who have positive energy. This workbook is designed to be a fun, interactive experience that will introduce this age group to simple ideas that can help create success in their lives.

Please keep in contact with us through our website at abundantspace.com. We will be advertising our workshops from the website. We offer consultations for your home, so please call us at 303-521-5213 to make arrangements. And feel free to offer any suggestions or ideas you may have. If you have any stories to share, please let us know so that we may add your story to a future book.

Author's Notes

There is a growing realization in the United States of the importance of the ancient Chinese philosophy of Feng Shui. As part of my organizational consulting business, I began to study these concepts and apply them to my personal life as well as the lives of my clients. It was amazing to see the transformation that occurred as a result of reorganizing environments in line with some simple, basic principles. As an excited new practitioner, I began to attend classes and workshops and achieved formal certification from the American Feng Shui Institute. I went on to attend the Feng Shui Certification Program Professional Training created by Master Yap Cheng Hai, studying form and shape, eight mansions and flying stars.

Opening my business Aisha Design, is an exciting time for me and I am enjoying my practice as it expands to many states. I plan to continue publishing a variety of articles to help explain these wonderful principles to a variety of audiences in simple, easy-to-use terms.

BIBLIOGRAPHY

Bruce, Ian. 1998. _Plan Your Home with Feng Shui_. Berkshire, England: Foulsham & Co. Ltd.

Carkhuff, R.R. 1969. _Helping and Human Relations: A Primer for Lay and Professional Helpers Vol. 2: Selection and Training_. Amherst, MA: Human Resource Development.

Chuen, Master Lam Kam 1996. _Feng Shui Handbook_. New York: Henry Holt

Englebert, Clear. 1999. _Bedroom Feng Shui_. Freedom, CA: The Crossing Press

Fretwell, Sally. 2000. _Feng Shui Back to Balance_. Charlottesville, VA Birthwrite Publishing

Hale, Gill. 1999. _Practical Encyclopedia of Feng Shui_. New York: Hermes House/Anness Publishing Limited

Jay, Roni. 1989 _Feng Shui in Your Garden_. Boston MA: Godsfield Press

Lim, Dr. Jess T.Y. 1999 _Feng Shui & Your Health_, Torrance, CA: Times Books International

Nowicki, Stephen. 1992. _Helping the Child Who Doesn't Fit In_. Atlanta, GA: Peachtree Press

0-595-26061-6

Printed in the United States
51560LVS00003B/56

9 780595 260614